Hi! Ho! The Rattlin' Bog

by John Langstaff and Beth and Joe Krush
THE SWAPPING BOY

by John Langstaff and Joe Krush
OL' DAN TUCKER

by John Langstaff and Feodor Rojankovsky
FROG WENT A-COURTIN'
(Caldecott Medal Winner)
OVER IN THE MEADOW

by John Langstaff and Antony Groves-Raines
ON CHRISTMAS DAY IN THE MORNING!

Hi! Ho! The Rattlin' Bog

and Other Folk Songs for Group Singing

SELECTED BY JOHN LANGSTAFF

with piano settings by
JOHN EDMUNDS · SEYMOUR BARAB
PHIL MERRILL · MARSHALL W. BARRON

with guitar chords suggested by
HAPPY TRAUM

Illustrated by Robin Jacques

HARCOURT, BRACE & WORLD, INC., NEW YORK

Preface

Here is a collection of folk songs, with infectious tunes, swinging rhythms, and catchy chorus refrains, particularly chosen for group singing. These songs, easy to pick up and fun to sing, have stood out as the favorites at all our "sings"—in classrooms and camps, in family groups, and on television on both sides of the Atlantic. They have proved so popular that for years I have been deluged with requests from teachers, parents, and the children themselves for a collection of the words and music. These are songs to be enjoyed at any age, for although I have used them particularly with children from the ages of eight to fourteen, I find that these same children as young people return to them years later with added delight.

The collection has been drawn from many sources: excerpts from various publications, books now out of print, and oral tradition. It is concerned with only one aspect of song, traditional music; but within this body of our anonymous and ever-changing music, we have represented a variety of moods and themes: sea chanteys and other work songs, lullabies, question-and-answer songs, folk hymns, counting songs, riddle songs, jig tunes, historical songs, simple part-songs, dance songs, narrative ballads, ghost songs, laments, calypso songs, and chorus songs to be led by a single voice. To give added variety, I asked four different musicians to tackle the settings, making the arrangements fresh and original, yet simple enough to play easily. Some of the tunes are unusual modal melodies, and in a few instances I have suggested that these be sung with no accompaniment. Actually, any of these songs can be sung *a cappella* to great effect. For those who prefer, basic guitar harmonies have been indicated.

To those boys and girls who have sung these songs with me over the years, to the teachers who have been my colleagues, and to my wife Nancy who is both teacher and collaborator, this book is affectionately dedicated.

JOHN LANGSTAFF

Some Hints for the Guitarist

In choosing the guitar chords for this collection, I have tried to do two things: keep the arrangements simple enough so that even a beginning guitarist can accompany these songs, and maintain a traditional feeling in the chord progressions. This means that occasionally the guitar and piano parts will differ, but they serve two very different functions. The piano arrangement is a composed setting and will be played, for the most part, as written. You, the guitarist, have only the chords to go by, and your accompaniment can be as simple or complex as you wish, using whatever strums, picks, bass runs, interludes, etc., that you have at your command. You can create your own accompaniment, whether it is the simplest strumming or the fanciest picking.

As with any instrument, certain keys present more of a problem to the novice than others. If you are a beginner, you will prefer those keys that enable you to play with a minimum of barred chords and long stretches. A, C, D, E, and G are the easiest keys on the guitar. You will find some songs in this book, however, which (for vocal range) have been set in the more "difficult" keys of F, B♭, and E♭. If this poses a problem for you, try using that ingenious device known as a *capo.* This is a clamp, sometimes made of metal, sometimes elastic, with a bar that presses down all six strings simultaneously at any given fret, thereby raising the pitch of the entire guitar. In this way, you can play a song in a familiar fingering but in a new key. For instance, if you place the capo at the third fret and finger a C chord above it, you will actually be playing an E♭ chord.

Certain songs, therefore, have been chorded two ways: the actual chord used, and (in parentheses) the alternate chord that you will use with the capo. At the end of the song you will be told at which fret to place the capo. For instance, look at "Wild Mountain Thyme" on page 100. At the end of the song it says "(capo III)." Place your capo at the third fret (make sure that it is on tight and doesn't buzz or rattle) and then play the chords in parentheses. Of course, if you aren't playing with another instrument, once you are familiar with the tune you can play those chords without a capo, or with the capo at *any* fret, depending on your own vocal range. Don't be afraid to experiment. The important thing is to play and sing these songs, and you will certainly enjoy them for a long, long time.

HAPPY TRAUM

Contents

Songs to Begin

Hi! Ho! The Rattlin' Bog

This is an Irish variant of an accumulative folk song that has roots in antiquity and is still sung traditionally in many parts of Europe, the United States, and Canada.

IRISH ACCUMULATIVE VARIANT
Arr. by Marshall W. Barron

As sung by Seamus Ennis, Dublin, Ireland.

11

rat-tlin' tree; The tree in the bog, And the bog down in the val-ley-O.

Hi! Ho! The rat-tlin' bog and the bog down in the val-ley-O,

Hi! Ho! The rat-tlin' bog and the bog down in the val-ley-O.

Fine

2. Now on this tree there was a limb, a rare limb, a

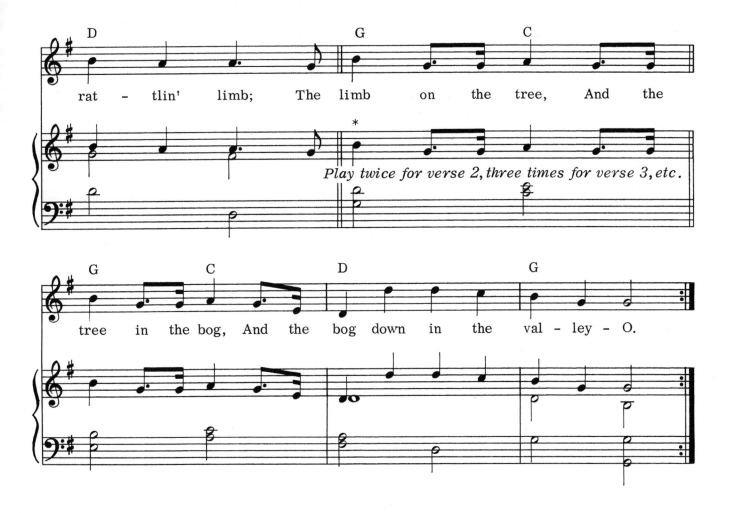

3. Now on this limb there was a branch, a rare branch, a rattlin' branch;
   The branch on the limb, and the limb on the tree,
   And the tree in the bog,
   And the bog down in the valley-O,
   Hi! Ho! The rattlin' bog and the bog down in the valley-O,
   Hi! Ho! The rattlin' bog and the bog down in the valley-O.

4. Now on this branch there was a nest, a rare nest, a rattlin' nest;
   The nest on the branch, *etc.*

5. Now in this nest there was an egg, a rare egg, a rattlin' egg;
   The egg in the nest, *etc.*

6. Now in this egg there was a bird, a rare bird, a rattlin' bird;
   The bird in the nest,
   The nest on the branch,
   The branch on the limb,
   The limb on the tree,
   The tree in the bog,
   And the bog down in the valley-O!
   Hi! Ho! The rattlin' bog and the bog down in the valley-O,
   Hi! Ho! The rattlin' bog and the bog down in the valley-O.

* This measure is repeated an additional time for each verse.

Dashing Away with the Smoothing Iron

FROM SOMERSET
Arr. by Phil Merrill

With a good swing ♩= 100

'Twas on a Mon – day morn – ing When I be–held my dar – ling, She

looked so neat and charm – ing In ev – 'ry high de – gree; —— She

*(For these chords, capo V)

14   From *A Selection of Collected Folk Songs* by Cecil Sharp and R. Vaughan Williams.
Reprinted by permission of Novello & Co., Ltd., London.

2. 'Twas on a Tuesday morning
   When I beheld my darling,
   She looked so neat and charming
   In ev'ry high degree;
   She looked so neat and nimble, O,
   A-starching of her linen, O.
   Dashing away with the smoothing iron,
   Dashing away with the smoothing iron,
   She stole my heart away.

3. Wednesday—A-hanging out.

4. Thursday—A-ironing.

5. Friday—A-folding.

6. Saturday—A-airing.

7. Sunday—A-wearing.

15

B for Barney

This street song was popular among Belfast weavers and spinners at the beginning of the century.

IRISH
Arr. by Seymour Barab

As sung by David Hammond, Belfast, North Ireland.

Three Craws

IRISH NONSENSE SONG
Arr. by Marshall W. Barron

3. The second craw up and flew awaw,
   Up and flew awaw, up and flew awaw,
   The second craw up and flew awaw,
   On a cold and frosty morning.

4. The third craw couldna' fly at all,
   Couldna' fly at all, couldna' fly at all,
   The third craw couldna' fly at all,
   On a cold and frosty morning.

5. The fourth craw wasn't there at all! *(End)*

The abrupt stop on the last stanza never fails to trip up the unwary singer, infected by the repetition and catchy tune!

17

Paper of Pins

UTAH VARIANT
Arr. by Marshall W. Barron

With a saucy lilt ♩.= 92

Boys: I'll give to you a pa-per of pins, For that's the way that love be-gins, If you will mar-ry me, me, me, If you will mar-ry me.____

Girls: I won't ac-cept your pa-per of pins, If that's the way that love be-gins, No,

*(For these chords, capo III)

18

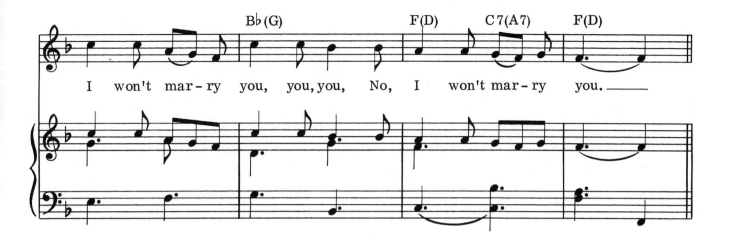

I won't mar-ry you, you, you, No, I won't mar-ry you._____

(Boys) 2. I'll give to you a dress of red,
      Stitched around with a golden thread,
      If you will marry me, me, me,
      If you will marry me.

(Girls)   I won't accept your dress of red,
      Stitched around with a golden thread,
      No, I won't marry you, you, you,
      No, I won't marry you.

   3. I'll give to you a rocking chair,
      Where you may sit to comb your hair, *etc.*

      I won't accept your rocking chair,
      Where I may sit to comb my hair, *etc.*

   4. I'll give to you the key to my heart,
      That you and I may never part, *etc.*

      I won't accept the key to your heart,
      That you and I may never part, *etc.*

   5. I'll give to you the key to my chest,
      That you can have money at your request, *etc.*

      I will accept the key to your chest,
      That I may have money at my request!
      Yes! I will marry you, you, you,
      Yes! I will marry you.

   6. Now I can see, as plain can be,
      You love my money, you don't love me.
      So I'll not marry you, you, you,
      So I'll not marry you!

Hill an' Gully

JAMAICAN
Arr. by Seymour Barab

*May be sung in two- or three-part harmony.

From *Folk Songs of Jamaica* by Tom Murray, Oxford University Press, London. Used by permission.

Candy Man

A solo voice lining out each short phrase at the beginning can vary the dynamics for the chorus to echo. Even if the tune is "free and easy," there should be a strict feeling of beat under it all. A light clap or a snap of the fingers on the offbeat will give the singing the necessary swing.

ADAPTED FROM A NEW ORLEANS BLUES
Arr. by Marshall W. Barron

give an-y-thing in this whole wide world If you bring my can-dy man home.

Go in-to the kit-chen, Get the ba-by some cake,—

Go in-to the kit-chen, Get the ba-by some cake,—

Go in-to the kit-chen, Get the ba-by some cake,—

Go in-to the kit-chen, Get the ba - by some cake, —

Go in-to the kit - chen, Get the ba - by some cake, —

Go in-to the kit - chen, Get the ba - by some cake, — I'd give an-y-thing in this

whole, wide world, If you bring my can - dy man home.

Processional and Ritual Songs

The Souling Song

For centuries this song has been chanted through lanes in Cheshire on All Souls' Day, as children went around the villages begging for pieces of the ritual Soul Cake. The basically three-note tune stems from the natural rise and fall of the human voice in primitive chant, calling, or street-cries.

FROM CHESHIRE
Arr. by Marshall W. Barron

Simply sung, at a walking tempo ♩. = 80

A

Soul! A Soul! A Soul - cake! Please, good Miss-is, a soul - cake! An

ap-ple, a pear, a plum or a cher-ry, An-y good thing to make us all mer-ry,

One for Pe - ter, two for Paul, Three for Him who made us all.

1. God bless the mas - ter of this house, The mis - ter - ess al - so; And
2. The lanes are ver - y dir - ty, My shoes are ver - y thin, I've

all the lit - tle chil - dren That 'round your ta - ble grow. Like -
got a lit - tle pock - et To put a pen - ny in. If you

wise young men and maid - ens, Your cat - tle and your store; And
have - n't got a pen - ny, A ha' - pen - ny will do; If you

all that dwells with - in your gates, We wish you ten times more. A
have - n't got a ha' - pen - ny, It's God bless you!

Unite and Unite

For centuries, on the first of May, the inhabitants of the little fishing village of Padstow, on the coast of Cornwall, have rushed out of their houses to join in this rousing processional. They follow as the ancient, ritual Hobby Horse, led by the magical "teaser" and surrounded by men of the village singing and playing accordions and drums, dances exuberantly through the streets. During the verse "O, where is St. George," the huge Horse sinks to the ground, miming the rite of dying; and a hush descends upon the crowd. Then, with the outburst of the chorus, the Hobby Horse leaps up again, symbolizing the renewing of life after the long winter, and the singing crowd surges on.

PADSTOW MAY SONG
Arr. by Phil Merrill

Rhythmic and energetic, with a slow heavy beat ♩ = 76

U - nite and u - nite, now let us u-nite, For sum-mer is a-come in to-day; And whi-ther we are go=ing, we all will u-nite, In the mer-ry morn-ing of May.

1. The young men of Padstow, they might if they would,
     For summer is a-come in today;
   They might have made a ship and gilded it with gold,
     In the merry morning of May!

2. The young girls of Padstow, they might if they would,
     For summer is a-come in today;
   They might have made a garland of the white rose and the red,
     In the merry morning of May!

3. O, where are the young men that now here would dance?
     For summer is a-come in today;
   O, some they are in England, and some they are in France,
     In the merry morning of May!

The verses above are sung to the same tune as the chorus. We suggest that "O, where is St. George" (see music on following page) be sung after the third verse, followed by a reprise of the chorus.

Mysteriously and very freely

O, where is St. George, O, where is he now? He's out in his long boat ____ All on ___ the salt ___ sea, O. Up flies the kite, Down falls the lark, O; Aunt Ur - su - la Bird-wood, She had an old ewe, And it died in her own ___ park, O. ____

dal Segno

The May Day Carol
(I've Been A-Wand'rin' All This Night)

This carol was originally sung as part of the custom on the first of May of gathering early spring flowers at dawn and leaving them on doorsteps in the village.

SPRING CAROL
Arr. by Marshall W. Barron

Smoothly, at a walking tempo ♩= 92

I've been a-wan-d'rin' all this night and the best part of the day, But when I come back home a-gain I will bring you a branch of May. A May.

2. A branch of May I bring you here,
   And at your door I stand,
   It's nothing but a sprout, but it's well budded out
   By the work of God's own hand.

3. My song is done, I must be gone,
   No longer can I stay;
   God bless you all, both great and small,
   And send you a joyful May.

The Wren Song

December 26, St. Stephen's Day, is still recognized traditionally in Ireland with this ancient song about the wren, the magical bringer of fire to the New Year. A group of boys, disguised and carrying a little caged effigy, vigorously sing this song from door to door.

IRISH RITUAL SONG
Arr. by Marshall W. Barron

The wren, the wren, the king of all birds, Saint
Ste-phen's Day was caught in the for-est. Al-though he was lit-tle, his
hon-or was great, Jump up, me lads, and give us a treat!

2. We followed the wren three miles or more,
   Three miles or more, three miles or more,
   Through hedges and ditches and heaps of snow,
   At six o'clock in the morning.

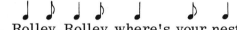

3. Rolley, Rolley, where's your nest?
   It's in the bush that I love best,
   It's in the bush, the holly tree,
   Where all the boys do follow me.

4. As I went out to hunt and all,
   I met a wren upon the wall,
   Up with me wattle and gave him a fall,
   And brought him here to show you all.

5. I have a little box under me arm,
   A tuppence or penny'll do it no harm,
   For we are the boys that came your way,
   To bring in the wren on St. Stephen's Day.

Dance Songs

Green Corn

1. All I want in this cre-a-tion Pret-ty lit-tle wife and a big plan-ta-tion, *Green corn,* *(clap hands)* *Green corn.*

1. *(clap hands)*
2. *(clap hands)*

2. Two little boys to call me Pappy,
One named Sop and the other named Gravy, *etc.*

Sourwood Mountain

SMOKEY MOUNTAIN VARIANT
Arr. by Marshall W. Barron

2. Raccoon canter and 'possum trot,
    Hay diddy ump, diddy iddy um day.
Black dog wrestle with a hickory knot,
    Hay diddy ump, diddy iddy um day.

3. Bring your old dog, get your gun, *etc.*
    Kill some game and have a little fun, *etc.*

4. Jaybird sitting on a hickory limb, *etc.*
    My six-foot rifle will sure get him, *etc.*

5. I got a gal in the head of the hollow, *etc.*
    She won't come and I won't follow, *etc.*

6. One of these days before very long, *etc.*
    I'll get that girl and a-home I'll run, *etc.*

38 From *English Folk Songs from the Southern Appalachians,* collected by Cecil Sharp, Oxford University Press, London.
Used by permission.

Jubilee!

KENTUCKY SINGING GAME
Arr. by Phil Merrill

*(For these chords, capo I)

2. Hardest work I ever done,
   Working on the farm,
   Easiest work I ever done,
   Swinging my true love's arm!

   Swing 'n' turn, Jubilee!
   Live 'n' learn, Jubilee!

3. Coffee grows on the white-oak tree,
   Sugar runs in brandy,
   Boys as pure as a lump of gold,
   Girls as sweet as candy!
   Refrain

4. If I had me a needle and thread,
   Fine as I could sew,
   Sew my true love to my side,
   And down this creek I'd go.
   Refrain

5. If I had no horse to ride,
   I'd be found a-crawling,
   Up and down this rocky road,
   Looking for my darling.
   Refrain

6. All out on the old railroad,
   'S'all out on the sea,
   'S'all out on the old railroad,
   Far as eye can see.
   Refrain

Mango Walk

FROM JAMAICA
Arr. by Seymour Barab

The girls may sing Verse 1 while the boys accompany them with this ostinato:

Man - go   walk_____

Verse 2 can be done with the girls accompanying the boys.

Give the Fiddler a Dram

Once you know this tune, try singing it at a good speed, unaccompanied, as "mouth music."

KENTUCKY FIDDLE TUNE
Arr. by Marshall W. Barron

Dance all night with your bot-tle in your hand, And long be-fore day give the fid-dler a dram, give the fid-dler a dram, give the fid-dler a dram, And long be-fore day give the fid-dler a dram.

*(For these chords, capo I)

42   From *English Folk Songs from the Southern Appalachians,* collected by Cecil Sharp, Oxford University Press, London.
Used by permission.

Some Say the Devil's Dead!

ENGLISH DANCE SONG
Arr. by Phil Merrill

With a strong beat and snap ♩.=120

Some say the dev-il's dead, the dev-il's dead, the dev-il's dead,

Some say the dev-il's dead and bu-ried in Cold Har - bour.

Some say he rose a - gain, some say he rose a - gain,

Some say he rose a-gain, and hir - ed to a bar - ber.

Clapping lightly on the <u>offbeat</u> gives the dance impetus.

I've Been to Haarlem

To play this singing game, couples of boys and girls promenade jauntily in a circle around any extra girls standing in the center. At "turn the glasses over," couples turn under their own crossed hands—away from each other. Then the boys continue circling single file, while the girls reverse directions and circle inside in the opposite direction—joined by the extra girls from the center. At the final note "o-*cean*," each boy grabs the nearest girl as his new partner, and the leftover girls go back to the middle of the ring of new couples as the song starts again.

AMERICAN SINGING GAME
Arr. by Phil Merrill

Easy-going walking pace ♩= 63

I've been to Haar-lem, I've been to Do - ver, I've trav-elled this wide world all o - ver; O - ver, o - ver, three times o - ver, Drink all the bran-dy wine and

Old Joe Clark

It's fun to take solo turns on the stanzas, with everybody joining in the chorus.

OZARK SQUARE-DANCE TUNE
Arr. by Phil Merrill

Old Joe Clark he had a house Fif-teen sto-ries high, And ev-ery sto-ry in that house Was filled with chick-en pie.

Refrain

Fare you well, old Joe Clark, Fare-well, Bet-sy Brown,

Fare you well, old Joe Clark, I'm gon-na leave this town.

2. I went down to old Joe's house,
   He invited me to supper,
   I stubbed my toe on the table leg
   And stuck my nose in the butter.

   > *Fare you well, old Joe Clark,*
   > *Farewell, Betsy Brown,*
   > *Fare you well, old Joe Clark,*
   > *I'm gonna leave this town.*

3. Old Joe Clark he had a mule,
   His name was Morgan Brown,
   And every tooth in that mule's head
   Was sixteen inches 'round.

   Refrain

4. I took my gal to the ball one night,
   I thought I'd have some fun,
   But all in the world that she would do
   Is sit and chew her gum.

   Refrain

5. I went down to Lexington,
   Didn't know the route,
   Put me in a coffee pot
   And poured me out the spout!

   Refrain

6. I wish I had a lariat rope,
   Long as I could throw,
   Throw it 'round my sweetheart's waist
   And down the road we'd go.

   Refrain

7. You go down the new-cut road,
   And I'll go down the lane,
   You can hug the old gatepost,
   And I'll hug Liza Jane.

   Refrain

Cripple Creek

"Mouth music" for dancing is used in many remote parts of the Appalachian Mountains. You don't need a phonograph or radio, or even a piano, to dance to music as long as your singing is rhythmic and infectious. You will like singing "Cripple Creek" without any accompaniment.

KENTUCKY MOUNTAIN DANCE-TUNE
Arr. by Phil Merrill

Crip - ple Creek girls, don't you want to go to So - mer-set?

So - mer-set girls, don't you want to go to town? So - mer-set girls, don't you

want to go to Crip-ple Creek? Cripple Creek girls, don't you want to go to town?

Try clapping lightly on the offbeat:

Clap!   Clap!

MacTavish

To the tune of "The Irish Washerwoman."

SCOTTISH "MOUTH MUSIC"
Arr. by Phil Merrill

Oh, ___ Mac-Ta-vish is dead and his broth-er don't know it, His broth-er is dead and Mac-Ta-vish don't know it, They're both of them dead and they're in the same bed, And nei-ther one knows that the o-ther is dead. Oh, Mac- other is dead!

Shady Grove

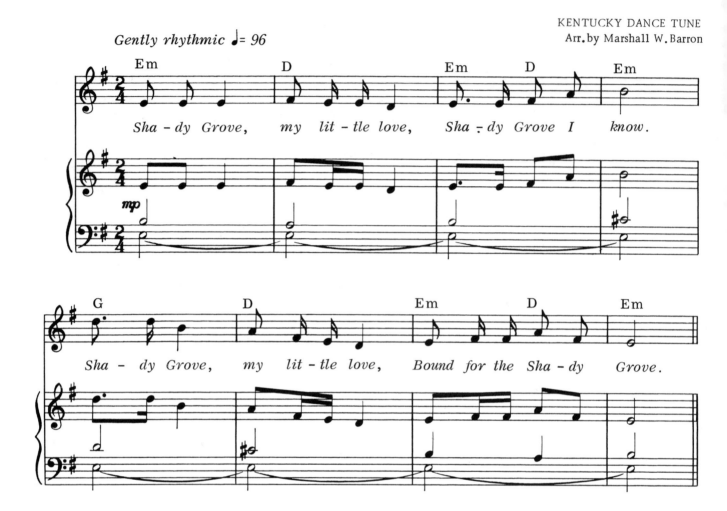

1. Cheeks as red as the blooming rose,
   Eyes of the deepest brown;
   You are the darling of my heart,
   Stay till the sun goes down.

   Shady Grove, my little love, etc.

2. Went to see my Shady Grove,
   Standing in the door;
   Shoes and stockings in her hand,
   Little bare feet on the floor.

   Shady Grove, my little love, etc.

3. Wisht I had a big fine horse,
   Corn to feed him on,
   Pretty little girl to stay at home,
   Feed him when I'm gone.

   Shady Grove, my little love, etc.

Ballads and Narrative Songs

The Bonny Banks of Virgie-O

Many of the traditional ballads contain short refrains within their stanzas, which make it easy to join in immediately as the story unfolds.

NEWFOUNDLAND BALLAD
Arr. by John Edmunds

Three fair maids went out for a walk; *All a lee and a lone-ly O,* They met a rob-ber on their way, *On the bon-ny, bon-ny banks of Vir-gie-O.* He— Vir-gie-O.

2. He took the first one by the hand
     All a lee and a lonely O,
   And he whipped her around and he made her stand
     On the bonny, bonny banks of Virgie-O.

3. O will you be a robber's wife?, *etc.*
   Or will you die by my penknife?, *etc.*

4. I will not be a robber's wife, *etc.*
   I would rather die by your penknife, *etc.*

5. O he took out his little penknife, *etc.*
   And it's then he took her own sweet life, *etc.*

6. He took the second one by the hand, *etc.*
   And he whipped her around and he made her stand, *etc.*

7. O will you be a robber's wife?, *etc.*
   Or will you die by my penknife?, *etc.*

8. I will not be a robber's wife, *etc.*
   I would rather die by your penknife, *etc.*

9. O he took out his little penknife, *etc.*
   And it's then he took her own sweet life, *etc.*

10. He took the third one by the hand, *etc.*
    And he whipped her around and he made her stand, *etc.*

11. O will you be a robber's wife?, *etc.*
    Or will you die by my penknife?, *etc.*

12. I will not be a robber's wife, *etc.*
    Nor will I die by your penknife, *etc.*

13. O if my brothers had been here, *etc.*
    You would not have killed my sisters dear, *etc.*

14. O where are your brothers, pray now tell?, *etc.*
    O one of them is a minister, *etc.*

15. And where is the other, pray now tell?, *etc.*
    He's out a-robbing like yourself, *etc.*

16. The Lord have mercy on my poor soul, *etc.*
    For I have killed my sisters dear, *etc.*

17. Then he took out his little penknife, *etc.*
    And it's then he took his own sweet life, *etc.*

The Bonny Earl o' Moray

In 1592, the Earl of Moray was cruelly murdered by the Earl of Huntly, supposedly to satisfy the King's jealousy of Moray, whom the Queen more rashly than wisely had commended in the King's hearing. The magnificent ruins of Doune Castle, where his lady waited in vain, still stand today. The game of "riding at the ring" is one in which the knight rode at full speed and tried to carry off, on the point of his lance, a ring or a glove suspended from some slight support.

SCOTTISH TRAGIC BALLAD
Arr. by John Edmunds

*(For these chords, capo III)

54

2. Now woe be to thee, Huntly,
And wherefore did ye so?
I bade ye bring him with ye,
But forbade ye him to slay.
He was a brave gallant,
And he played at the glove;
And the bonny Earl o' Moray,
He was the Queen's own love.

O long will his lady
Look o'er from Castle Doune,
Ere she see the Earl o' Moray
Come soundin' through the toon!   (town)

Carrion Crow

Clear, crisp enunciation of the words of the nonsense refrains gives a marvelous rhythmic sound.

TENNESSEE NONSENSE SONG
Arr. by Marshall W. Barron

From *Seventeen Nursery Songs from the Appalachian Mountains,* collected by Cecil Sharp.
Reprinted by permission of Novello & Co., Ltd., London.

2. Wife, O wife, bring hither my bow,
     With a ling dong dilly dol kiro me
  That I may shoot this carrion crow,
     With a ling dong dilly dol kiro me.
     Hi falero gil fin a garo
     Hi falero gil fin a gay.
     Up jumped Johnny a-ringing of his bell,
     With a ling dong dilly dol kiro me.

3. The tailor shot and he missed his mark, *etc.*
  And shot his old sow bang through the heart, *etc.*

4. Wife, O wife, bring brandy in a spoon, *etc.*
  The old sow's fallen down in a swoon, *etc.*

5. The old sow died and the bells did toll, *etc.*
  And the little pigs squeaked for the old sow's soul, *etc.*

Cock Robin

This seemingly nonsensical song has primitive roots far back in animal worship and sacrifice. When sung softly and slowly by a large group, the tune has a mesmerizing effect!

FROM NORTH CAROLINA
Arr. by John Edmunds

Who killed cock_ rob - in? Who killed cock_ rob - in?

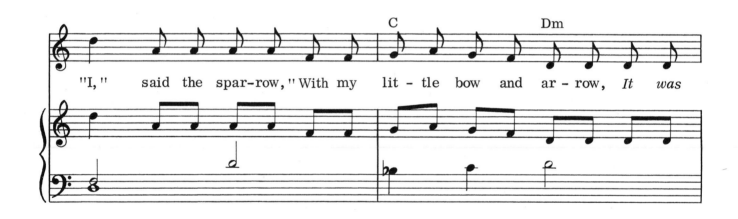

"I," said the spar-row, "With my lit - tle bow and ar - row, It was

I, Oh,— it was I." I."

Collected by Richard Chase from an Appalachian singer on White Top Mountain.

2. Who saw him die?
     Who saw him die?
   "I," said the fly,
   "With my little teensy eye,
     It was I,
     Oh, it was I."

3. Who caught his blood?, *etc.*
   "I," said the fish, "with my little silver dish," *etc.*

4. Who made his coffin?, *etc.*
   "I," said the snipe, "with my little pocket knife," *etc.*

5. Who made his shrouden?, *etc.*
   "I," said the beetle, "with my little sewing needle," *etc.*

6. Who dug his grave?, *etc.*
   "I," said the crow, "with my little spade and hoe," *etc.*

7. Who let him down?, *etc.*
   "I," said the crane, "with my little golden chain," *etc.*

8. Who pat his grave?, *etc.*
   "I," said the duck, "with my big old splatter foot," *etc.*

9. Who preached his funeral?, *etc.*
   "I," said the swallow, "just as loud as I could holler!" *etc.*

As I Walked Through London City

FROM ESSEX
Arr. by John Edmunds

Lightly, with gusto ♩= 84

F(D)*

As I walked through Lon-don Ci - ty,

Gm(Em)   C(A)   F(D)

Af - ter twelve o' -clock at night, There I saw a Span-ish la - dy

Bb(G)   F(D)   C7(A7) F(D)   *Refrain* F(D)

wash - ing and iron - ing by can - dle - light. *Fal the ral the*

*(For these chords, capo III)

60

2. Madam, I have come to court you
   If your favour I should win;
   If you make me kindly welcome
   Then perhaps I'll come again.

   Fal the ral the riddle all the raydo,
   Fal the ral the riddle all the day,
   Fal the ral the riddle all the raydo,
   Fal lal la the riddle all the day.
   Twenty, eighteen, sixteen, fourteen,
   Twelve, ten, eight, six, four, two, none;
   Nineteen, seventeen, fifteen, thirteen,
   'Leven, nine, seven, five, three and one.

3. Madam, I've got rings and jewels,
   Madam, I've got house and land,
   Madam, I've the world of treasure,
   If you'll be at my command.

   Refrain

4. What care I for your rings and jewels,
   What care I for your house and land,
   What care I for your world of treasure,
   All I want is a handsome man.

   Refrain

Sea Songs

Fire! Fire!

A sea chantey was the sailors' work song in the days of sailing vessels. A good chanteyman was a valuable member of the crew. He kept the sailors amused and made the work more efficient by his rhythmic leadership. The key to good chantey rhythm is to make it reluctant—the "pull" should be strongly felt in the sailors' chorus line. In most chanteys, the final notes of each chorus should be held out until the chanteyman enters again—so there are no gaps!

PUMPING CHANTEY
Arr. by Phil Merrill

Deliberately, with a strong heavy beat ♩= 76

Chanteyman:
There's a fire in the gal-ley, There's a fire down be-low,
Fetch a buck-et of wa - ter, girls, There's fire down be - low.

Chorus
Fire! Fire! Fire down be - low. It's

fetch a buck-et of wa-ter, girls, There's fire down be-low!

2. There's a fire in the foretop,
   There's a fire in the main;
   Fetch a bucket of water, girls,
   And put it out again.

   Fire! Fire! Fire down below.
   It's fetch a bucket of water, girls,
   There's fire down below!

3. There's a fire to the starboard,
   There's a fire in the stern.
   Fetch a bucket of water, girls,
   Let's give the pump a turn.

   Chorus

4. As I walked out one morning fair
   All in the month of June,
   I overheard an Irish girl
   A-singing this old tune.

   Chorus

Ballinderry

NORTH IRELAND
Arr. by Seymour Barab

Smooth and flowing ♩.= 50

1. 'Tis pret-ty to be in Bal - lin-der-ry,
of-ten I sailed to bon-ny Rams Is-land,

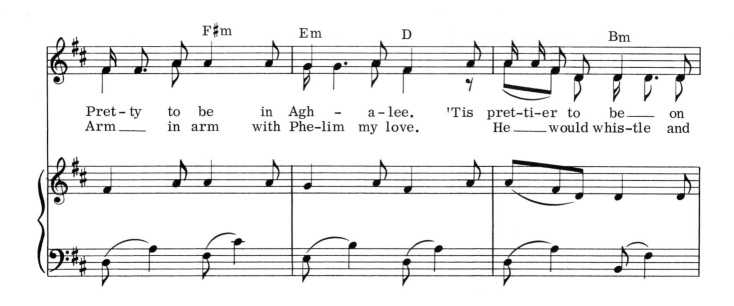

Pret-ty to be in Agh - a-lee. 'Tis pret-ti-er to be___ on
Arm___ in arm with Phe-lim my love. He___ would whis-tle and

bon-ny Rams Is-land, A-sit-ting for-ev-er be-neath a tree. *Och on*
I — would sing— And we — would make the whole is-land ring.

och — on   och   on   och — on. 2.For   och — on.

3. 'Tis pretty to be in Ballinderry,
   But now it's sad as sad can be,
   For the ship that sailed with Phelim, my demon,
   Is sunk forever beneath the sea.

   Och on och on
   Och on och on.

If you want to sing this unaccompanied, you can add a second part under the melody,
repeating, over and over:

Och   on   och   on   on.——

Won't You Go My Way?

Manual work aboard ship in the days of sail was strenuous and heavy. Remember this when you want to get the feeling of rhythmic pulse into the singing of these work songs!

HALYARD CHANTEY
Arr. by Marshall W. Barron

With marked heaviness ♩ = 104

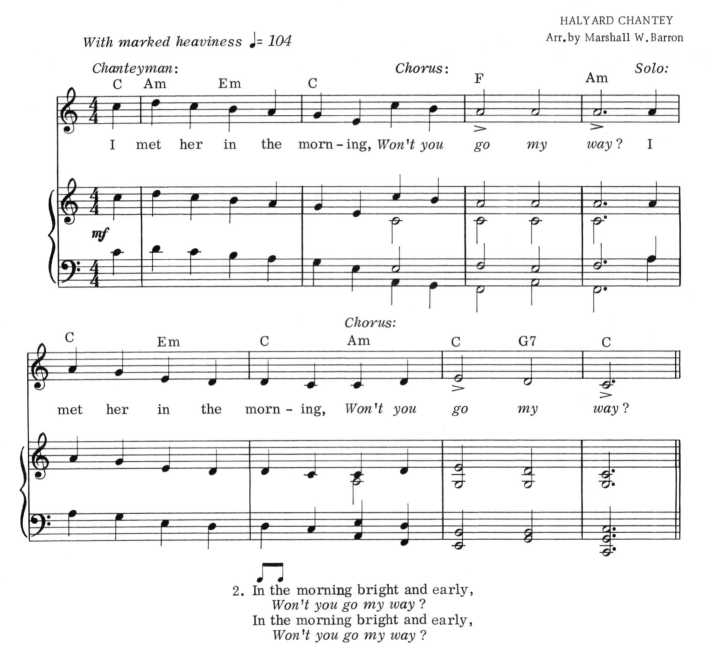

2. In the morning bright and early,
   Won't you go my way?
   In the morning bright and early,
   Won't you go my way?

3. Oh, Julia, Anna, Maria, *etc.*

4. I asked that girl to marry, *etc.*

5. She said she'd rather tarry, *etc.*

6. Oh, marry, never tarry, *etc.*

Haul Away, Joe!

This chantey is used for raising the foresail, with a sudden strong pull on the last word each time. The chanteyman's solo can be very free while the sailors ready themselves for the next pull, but the chorus must be powerfully rhythmic.

SHORT-HAUL CHANTEY
Arr. by Marshall W. Barron

Strong and heavy ♩= 58

Chanteyman:

Oh, when I was a lit-tle boy, And so my moth-er told me,

Chorus:

'Way, haul a-way, we'll haul a-way, Joe! (shout)

2. That if I did not kiss the girls
   My lips would all grow moldy,
   'Way, haul away, we'll haul away, Joe!

3. Once I was in Ireland
   A-digging turf and praties, *etc.*

4. But now I'm on a Yankee ship
   A-hauling sheets and braces, *etc.*

5. 'Way, haul away,
   We'll haul away together, *etc.*

6. 'Way, haul away,
   We'll haul for better weather, *etc.*

7. King Louis was the King of France
   Before the Revolution, *etc.*

8. But then he got his head cut off,
   Which spoiled his constitu-shi-en, *etc.*

Mingulay Boat Song

Mingulay is one of the outer islands of the Hebrides, off Scotland. The Minch is the treacherous body of water that must be crossed to reach Mingulay.

HEBRIDEAN SEA SONG
Arr. by Seymour Barab

*(For these chords, capo III)

My Bonny Lad

SCOTS' LAMENT
Arr. by Seymour Barab

*May be sung throughout as a drone accompaniment.

Leave Her, Johnny

This chantey was sung while the sailors tramped around the capstan to raise or lower the anchor, led by the chanteyman's grumbling verses about the homeward-bound journey.

CAPSTAN CHANTEY
Arr. by Marshall W. Barron

2. The bread is hard and the beef is salt,
   Leave her, Johnny, leave her,
   The bread is hard and the beef is salt,
   It's time for us to leave her.

3. O, a leaking ship and a harping crew, *etc.*

4. I've got no money, I've got no clothes, *etc.*

5. O, my old mother she wrote to me, *etc.*

6. I will send you money, I will send you clothes, *etc.*

From *English Folk Chanteys,* collected by Cecil Sharp, Novello & Co., Ltd., London.
Reprinted by permission of the Cecil Sharp Estate.

I'se the B'y That Builds the Boat

The refrain of this catchy dance tune includes the tongue-twisting names of local harbors.

NEWFOUNDLAND DANCE SONG
Arr. by John Edmunds

I'se the b'y that builds the boat, And I'se the b'y that sails her. I'se the b'y that catch-es the fish, And takes 'em home to 'Li - zer.

Refrain:
Hip yer part - ner, Sal - ly Tibbs. Hip yer part - ner, Sal - ly Brown.

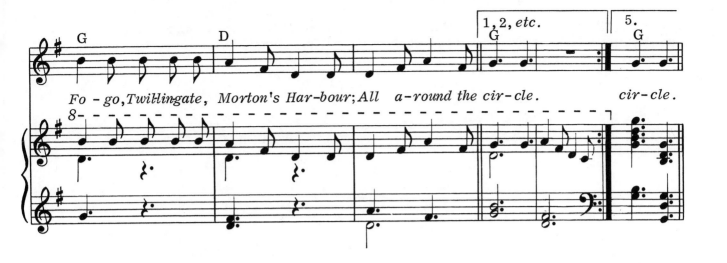

Fo - go, Twillingate, Morton's Har-bour; All a-round the cir-cle.

cir-cle.

2. Sods and rinds to cover your flake,
   Cake and tea for supper;
   Codfish in the spring of the year,
   Fried in maggoty butter!

   Hip yer partner, Sally Tibbs.
   Hip yer partner, Sally Brown.
   Fogo, Twillingate, Morton's Harbour;
   All around the circle.

3. I don't want your maggoty fish,
   That's no good for winter;
   I could buy as good as that
   Down in Bonavista.

   Refrain

4. I took 'Lizer to a dance,
   And faith! but she could travel!
   Ev'ry step that she did take
   Was up to her knees in gravel!

   Refrain

5. Susan White she's out of sight,
   Her petticoat needs a border.
   Old Sam Oliver in the dark,
   He kissed her in the corner!

   Refrain

Paddy Doyle

Bunting a sail took one strenuous heave to lift the heavy, rolled canvas aloft. The chantey is a good example of how these work songs evolved out of the natural rhythm of pulling and releasing—groans and grunts!

BUNTING CHANTEY
Arr. by Marshall W. Barron

Very slowly and heavily ♩= 84

To my way ____ ay ____ ay! ____ We'll pay Pad-dy Doyle for his boots!

To my way ____ ay ____ ay! ____ We'll all shave un-der the chin!

(grunt!) (shout!) (grunt!) (shout!)

76

Shanandar

Sailors liked the exotic sound of "Shanandar," a mispronunciation of an Indian chief's name: Shanandoah.

CAPSTAN CHANTEY
Arr. by Marshall W. Barron

2. Oh, Shanandar, I love your daughter,
    'Way-ay, you rolling river!
Oh, Shanandar, I love your daughter,
    'Way-ay, we're bound away,
    'Cross the wide Missouri.

3. For seven long years I courted Sally, *etc.*

4. And seven more I couldn't gain her, *etc.*

5. She said I was a tarry sailor, *etc.*

6. Farewell, my dear, I'm bound to leave you, *etc.*
    I'm bound away, but will ne'er deceive you, *etc.*

Supernatural and Ghost Songs

Skin and Bones

KENTUCKY GHOST SONG
Arr. by Marshall W. Barron

Deadpan and eerie ♩.= 46

1. There was an old wom-an all skin and bones,

oo - oo - oo! ____
2. She lived down by the old grave-yard,
3. One night she thought she'd take a walk,

oo - oo - oo! _____ 4. She walked down by the old grave-yard,
oo - oo - oo! _____ 5. She saw the bones a - lying a - round,

oo - oo - oo! _____ 6. She went to the clos-et to get a broom,

oo - oo - oo! _____ 7. She op-ened the door and BOO!

(All white notes)

(All black notes)

Sinner Man

This powerful tune, rather like a sea chantey, has a text of colorful imagery. It can be effectively divided between solo voices and chorus.

APPALACHIAN MOUNTAIN VARIANT
Arr. by John Edmunds

O sin-ner man, where are you going to run to? O sin-ner man, where are you going to run to? O sin-ner man, where are you going to run to? O sin-ner man, where are you going to run to

All — on that day? Run to the sun: O sun, won't you hide me?

Run to the sun: O sun, won't you hide me? Run to the sun: O sun, won't you hide me?

82   From *English Folk Songs from the Southern Appalachians,* collected by Cecil Sharp, Oxford University Press, London.
Used by permission.

2. *Refrain.*
   Run to the moon: O moon, won't you hide me?
   Run to the moon: O moon, won't you hide me?
   Run to the moon: O moon, won't you hide me
   All on that day?
   The Lord said: O sinner man, the moon'll be a-bleeding.
   The Lord said: O sinner man, the moon'll be a-bleeding.
   The Lord said: O sinner man, the moon'll be a-bleeding
   All on that day.

3. *Refrain.*
   Run to the stars: O stars, won't you hide me?, *etc.*
   The Lord said: O sinner man, the stars'll be a-falling, *etc.*

4. *Refrain.*
   Run to the sea: O sea, won't you hide me?, *etc.*
   The Lord said: O sinner man, the sea'll be a-sinking, *etc.*

5. *Refrain.*
   Run to the rocks: O rocks, won't you hide me?, *etc.*
   The Lord said: O sinner man, the rocks'll be a-rolling, *etc.*

6. *Refrain.*
   Run to the Lord: O Lord, won't you hide me?, *etc.*
   The Lord said: O sinner man, you ought to been a-praying, *etc.*

7. *Refrain.*
   Sinner man says: Lord, I've been a-praying, *etc.*
   The Lord said: O sinner man, you prayed too late, *etc.*

8. *Refrain.*
   Run to Satan: O Satan, won't you hide me?, *etc.*
   Satan said: O sinner man, step right in!, *etc.*

The Devil's Questions

In this type of ballad, a highly dramatic story of confrontation is told solely through dialogue. In such ballads, if a victim can outwit the evil questioner, he is saved.

FROM VIRGINIA
Arr. by Seymour Barab

1. If you can't an-swer my ques - tions nine, *Sing*
10. Now you have an-swered my ques - tions nine. *Sing*

nine - ty-nine and nine - ty! ____ Oh, you're not God's, you're
nine - ty-nine and nine - ty! ____ Oh, you are God's, you're

one of mine. And you're not the weav - er's bon - ny. ____
none of mine. And you *are* the weav - er's bon - ny. ____ *Fine*

*(For these chords, capo V)

Collected by Richard Chase from a singer near Chapel Hill, North Carolina.

2. Oh, what is high-er than the tree? *Sing*
nine - ty - nine and nine-ty! And what is deep - er
than the sea? And you're not the weav-er's bon- ny. 3. Oh
heav'n is high-er than the tree, *Sing* nine-ty-nine and nine-ty! And

hell is deep - er than the sea, And I am the weav-er's bon - ny.

After stanza 9,
D.C. al Fine

4. Oh, what is whiter than the milk?
    Sing ninety-nine and ninety!
   And what is softer than the silk?
    And you're not the weaver's bonny.

5. Oh, snow is whiter than the milk, *etc.*
   And down is softer than the silk,
    And I am the weaver's bonny.

6. Oh, what is louder than the horn?, *etc.*
   And what is sharper than the thorn?
    And you're not the weaver's bonny.

7. Oh, thunder is louder than the horn, *etc.*
   And hunger's sharper than the thorn,
    And I am the weaver's bonny.

8. Oh, what's more innocent than a lamb?, *etc.*
   And what is meaner than womankind?
    And you're not the weaver's bonny.

9. A babe's more innocent than a lamb, *etc.*
   And the Devil is meaner than womankind!
    And I am the weaver's bonny.

10. Now you have answered my questions nine, *etc.*
    Oh, you are God's, you're none of mine,
     And you are the weaver's bonny.

As I Was Going to Banbury

FROM BERKSHIRE
Arr. by John Edmunds

2. And when the apples began to fall,
    Ri fol lat-i-tee O,
  And when the apples began to fall,
  I found five hundred men in all,
    With a ri fol lat-i-tee O.

3. And one of the men I saw was dead, *etc.*
  So I sent for a hatchet to open his head, *etc.*

4. And in his head I found a spring, *etc.*
  And seven young salmon a-learning to sing, *etc.*

5. And one of the salmon as big as I, *etc.*
  Now do you think I am telling a lie?, *etc.*

6. And one of the salmon as big as an elf, *etc.*
  If you want any more you must sing it yourself!, *etc.*

The Gray Goose

The verses may be sung as solos, with everybody joining in the chorus on *Lawd, Lawd, Lawd*.

LOUISIANA "TALL TALE"
Arr. by Seymour Barab

*(For these chords, capo I)

2. He went to the big wood,
     Lawd, Lawd, Lawd,
   An' took along his shotgun,
     Lawd, Lawd, Lawd.

3. 'Long come a gray goose, *etc.*
   Well, up to his shoulder, *etc.*

4. He rammed back the hammer, *etc.*
   An' he pulled on the trigger, *etc.*

5. The gun went off "boo-loom," *etc.*
   Down came the gray goose, *etc.*

6. Down he came a-fallin', *etc.*
   He was six weeks a-fallin', *etc.*

7. Then your wife and my wife, *etc.*
   They gave it feather pickin', *etc.*

8. They were six weeks a-pickin', *etc.*
   An' they set him on the par-boil, *etc.*

9. He was six weeks a-boilin', *etc.*
   An' they put him on the table, *etc.*

10. And the fork couldn't stick him, *etc.*
    An' the knife couldn't cut him, *etc.*

11. Well, they throw'd him in the hog pen, *etc.*
    An' the hog couldn't eat him, *etc.*

12. He broke the hog's teeth out, *etc.*
    So they took him to the sawmill, *etc.*

13. The saw couldn't cut him, *etc.*
    An' he broke the saw's teeth out, *etc.*

14. And the last time I seed him, *etc.*
    He was flyin' cross the ocean, *etc.*

15. With a long stream of goslin's, *etc.*
    An' they all gwine "quonk, quonk," *etc.*

Soldier Songs

Doodle Dandy

Old-timers in upper New York State say that this was sung by the American troops as they marched down the Hudson to take over New York City after the evacuation of the British.

BANJO TUNE FROM THE AMERICAN REVOLUTION
Arr. by Marshall W. Barron

Guitar accompaniment, rhythmical strumming:

Collected and recorded by Frank Warner.

And ev-'ry Yan-kee will have on his back, a great big pump-kin in his sack, A lit-tle mo-las-ses and a piece of pork, and a-way we'll march straight for New York.

Johnny Has Gone for a Soldier

Originally this poignant tune came with the early settlers from Ireland and, during the American Revolution, gained a great deal of popularity among the soldiers. The nonsense chorus derives from the sounds of the original Gallic words whose meaning was lost in the transfer across the ocean.

CATSKILL MOUNTAIN VARIANT
Arr. by Seymour Barab

Smooth and flowing ♩= 100

1. Here I sit on But-ter-milk Hill, Who could blame me
sell my clock, I'd sell my reel. Like-wise I'd sell my

cry my fill? And ev-ery tear would turn a mill;
spin-ning wheel To buy my love a sword of steel;

Refrain:

John-ny has gone for a sol - dier.
John-ny has gone for a sol - dier. *Shoo - lie, shoo - lie, shoo-lie__too,*

shoo - lie, sac-car-ac-ca bib-ba-lib-ba-boo, If I should die for

sal-ly bo-bo-link, come bib-ba-lib-ba-boo sa-ro - ra. 2.I'd ro - ra.

Soldier Boy
(Walking on the Green Grass)

FROM VIRGINIA
Arr. by John Edmunds

*(For these chords, capo III)

 From *Seventeen Nursery Songs from the Appalachian Mountains,* collected by Cecil Sharp.
Reprinted by permission of Novello & Co., Ltd., London.

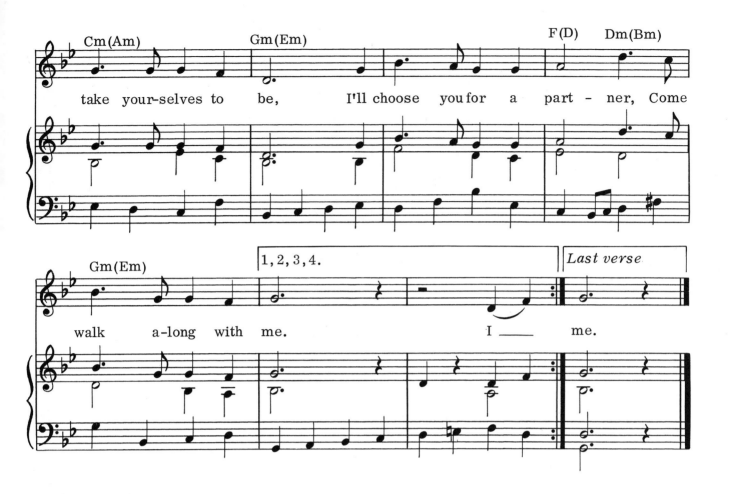

take your-selves to be, I'll choose you for a part - ner, Come

walk a-long with me. I ___ me.

(Girls) 2. I would not marry a blacksmith;
He smuts his nose and chin.
I'd rather marry a soldier boy
That marches through the wind.
Soldier boy, O soldier boy,
Soldier boy for me.
If ever I get married,
A soldier's wife I'll be.

3. I would not marry a doctor;
He's always killing the sick.
I'd rather marry a soldier boy
That marches double quick.
Soldier boy, O soldier boy,
Soldier boy for me.
If ever I get married,
A soldier's wife I'll be.

4. I would not marry a farmer;
   He's always selling grain.
   I'd rather marry a soldier boy
   That marches through the rain.
   Soldier boy, O soldier boy,
   Soldier boy for me.
   If ever I get married,
   A soldier's wife I'll be.

(Boys) We go walking on the green grass,
        Thus, thus, thus.
        Come, all you pretty fair maids,
        Come walk along with us.
        So pretty and so fair
        As you take yourselves to be,
        I'll choose you for a partner,
        Come walk along with me.

Suggestion for singing a cappella:

(Note: The single bass line in the piano accompaniment could be added to this with a cello or guitar.)

98

Part Songs

Wild Mountain Thyme

The men of the McPeake family, from whom this song was collected, often accompany them-selves on the bagpipe, which influences their singing and harmony.

NORTH IRELAND
Arr. by Phil Merrill

Sustained, and with feeling ♩=46

O, the sum-mer time is com-ing, And the trees are sweet-ly bloom-ing, And the wild moun-tain thyme— Grows a -

*(For these chords, capo III)

2. I will build my love a tower,
   By yon clear crystal fountain,
   And on it I will pile
   All the flowers of the mountain.
   Will you go, lassie, go?
   Refrain

3. If my true love she was gone,
   I would surely find no other
   To pull wild mountain thyme
   All around the purple heather.
   Will you go, lassie, go?
   Refrain

Sheep-Shearing Song

ADAPTATION OF AN ENGLISH FOLK SONG
Arr. by Marshall W. Barron

*(For these chords, capo I)

2. The sixth month of the year,
   In the month calléd June,
   When the weather's too hot to be borne,
   The master doth say,
   As he goes on his way:
   "Tomorrow my sheep shall be shorn,
   Tomorrow my sheep shall be shorn."

3. Now, the sheep they're all shorn,
   And the wool carried home,
   Here's a health to our master and flock;
   And if we should stay,
   Till the last goes away,
   I'm afraid 'twill be past twelve o'clock,
   I'm afraid 'twill be past twelve o'clock.

While Shepherds Watched Their Flocks by Night
(On Ilkla Moor Baht Hat)

The Yorkshire town of Ilkley is known among folk singers in the humorous song, "On Ilkla Moor Baht Hat," the traditional words of which are included below. However, this same tune has been sung at Christmas throughout the sheep country of Yorkshire and Lancastershire to the familiar words of Nahum Tate.

YORKSHIRE TRADITIONAL TUNE
Arr. by Marshall W. Barron

* (For these chords, capo III)

2. "Fear not," said he, for mighty dread (mighty dread)
      Had seized their troubled mind;
   "Glad tidings of great joy I bring (Glad tidings of great joy I bring)
   Glad tidings of great joy I bring (Glad tidings of great joy I bring)
      To you and all mankind (mankind),
      To you and all mankind (mankind),
      To you and all mankind.

3. "To you, in David's town this day (town, this day)
      Is born of David's line,
   The Saviour, Who is Christ the Lord, *etc.*
      And this shall be the sign (the sign), *etc.*

4. "The heavenly Babe you there shall find (there shall find)
      To human view displayed,
   All meanly wrapped in swathing bands, *etc.*
      And in a manger laid (manger laid)," *etc.*

5. Thus spake the seraph, and forthwith (and forthwith)
      Appeared a shining throng
   Of angels praising God, who thus, *etc.*
      Addressed their joyful song (joyful song), *etc.*

6. "All glory be to God on high (God on high)
      And on the earth be peace;
   Goodwill henceforth from heaven to men, *etc.*
      Begin and never cease (never cease)," *etc.*

On Ilkla Moor Baht* Hat

1. Where hast thou been since I saw thee (I saw thee)
      On Ilkla Moor baht hat?
   Where hast thou been since I saw thee
                           (Where hast thou been since I saw thee)
   Where hast thou been since I saw thee
                           (Where hast thou been since I saw thee)
   On Ilkla Moor baht hat (baht hat),
   On Ilkla Moor baht hat (baht hat),
   On Ilkla Moor baht hat?

2. I've been a-courtin' Mary Jane (Mary Jane)
      On Ilkla Moor baht hat, *etc.*

3. There wilt thou catch thy death of cold (death of cold), *etc.*

4. Then we will come and bury thee (bury thee), *etc.*

5. Then worms will come and eat thee up (eat thee up), *etc.*

6. Then ducks will come and eat up worms (eat up worms), *etc.*

7. Then we will come and eat up ducks (eat up ducks), *etc.*

8. Then us will all have et up thee! (et up thee!), *etc.*

*("Baht" means "without.")

Wondrous Love

Among the traditional folk hymns of America, this noble tune stands out as one of the grandest. It is found in the early American *Shape-Note Hymnal*, but its roots can be traced back as far as the sixteenth century.

AMERICAN FOLK HYMN
Arr. by John Edmunds

Sustained, but with exultation ♩ = 88

1. What won-drous love is this, O my soul, O my soul! What
2. To God and to the Lamb I will sing, I will sing, to

won-drous love is this, O my soul! _____ What
God and to the Lamb I will sing. _____ To

won - drous love is this, That caused the Lord _ of bliss To
God and to the Lamb Who is the great _ I AM, While

send this per - fect peace to my soul, to my soul, To
mil - lions join the theme, I will sing, I will sing, While

send this per - fect peace to my soul.
mil - lions join the theme I will sing.

Alternate version of "Wondrous Love" for three parts, *a cappella*

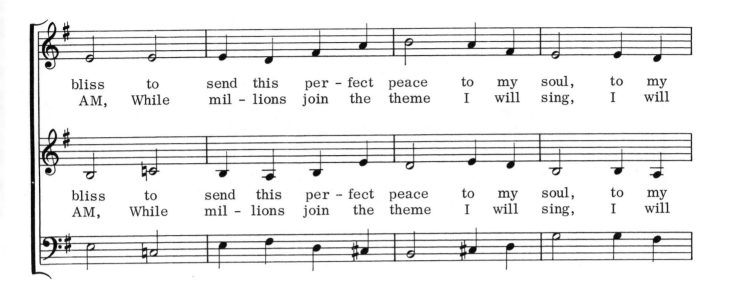

bliss to send this per - fect peace to my soul, to my
AM, While mil - lions join the theme I will sing, I will

bliss to send this per - fect peace to my soul, to my
AM, While mil - lions join the theme I will sing, I will

soul, To send this per - fect peace to my soul.
sing, While mil - lions join the theme I will sing.

soul, To send this per - fect peace to my soul.
sing, While mil - lions join the theme I will sing.

INDEX OF TITLES